BRIGHT
IDEA
BOOKS

YOU CAN WORK IN Movies

by Samantha S. Bell

raintree
a Capstone company — publishers for children

Raintree is an imprint of Capstone Global Library Limited, a company incorporated in England and Wales having its registered office at 264 Banbury Road, Oxford, OX2 7DY – Registered company number: 6695582

www.raintree.co.uk
myorders@raintree.co.uk

Edited by Charly Haley
Designed by Becky Daum
Production by Claire Vanden Branden
Originated by Capstone Global Library Ltd
Printed and bound in India

ISBN 978 1 4747 7532 8 (hardback)
22 21 20 19 18
10 9 8 7 6 5 4 3 2 1

ISBN 978 1 4747 7356 0 (paperback)
22 21 20 19 18
10 9 8 7 6 5 4 3 2 1

British Library Cataloguing in Publication Data
A full catalogue record for this book is available from the British Library.

Acknowledgements
We would like to thank the following for permission to reproduce photographs: iStockphoto: andresr, 5, bjones27, 8–9, 11, 26–27, ContentWorks, 30–31, hiphunter, 21, philipimage, 17, powerofforever, 13; Shutterstock Images: 2p2play, cover (foreground), antb, 6, bepsy, 29, gnepphoto, cover (background), Gorodenkoff, 24–25, guruXOX, 14–15, 18–19, panuwat phimpha, 23. Design Elements: iStockphoto, Red Line Editorial, and Shutterstock Images.

Every effort has been made to contact copyright holders of material reproduced in this book. Any omissions will be rectified in subsequent printings if notice is given to the publisher.

CONTENTS

CHAPTER 1

PRODUCERS

The lights go down. The cinema is dark. The movie starts! It lasts a couple of hours. But it took a long time to make.

4

At the end of the movie is a list of **credits**. These are the names of all the people who helped make the movie. Some movies have hundreds of people working on them.

Only the biggest movies are shown in cinemas everywhere. Some movies are made for TV. Others are shown at small cinemas.

Producers choose the story. It may be a new **script**. It may be from a book. Sometimes it is a true story. Producers buy the **rights**. The rights let them work with the story. Then they can make the movie.

A person usually works in different movie jobs before becoming a producer.

WRITING A MOVIE

Screenwriters write scripts. They create stories and characters. They write **lines** for the actors to say.

Movies cost a lot to make. Producers keep track of the money. They also hire the **director**. Sometimes they hire the actors too.

The team that helps a producer is called a film crew.

Some producers work on big movies. They have a team to help them. Some work on small movies. They may do the job alone.

Many producers studied film at university. Some have had business training.

CHAPTER 2

DIRECTORS

Directors find the best way to show the story in a movie. They also decide who works on the movie. They go to **rehearsals** and help the actors. Directors also work with **composers** to make the music. It may take months or years to finish a movie.

Most directors start with small movies or theatre plays. Then they may move on to bigger movies.

A director is in charge during filming.

CHAPTER 3

ACTORS

Actors play the characters in movies. They may change the way they look to fit their characters.

They remember lines. They practise **scenes**. They try to make the characters seem real.

Actors practise a lot. They want to be ready when it's time for filming.

Sometimes actors work inside a movie studio. Sometimes they work outside. They may film in another country.

Many actors have **agents**. Agents help actors to find **roles** in movies. Most actors must **audition** for roles.

Some actors study drama at university or college. Others take acting lessons. Many actors start by working as extras. Extras are actors in the backgrounds of movies. They don't usually have lines.

STUNTS

Stuntmen and stuntwomen replace actors for dangerous scenes.

CHAPTER 4

FILM CREW Members

Crew members work behind the scenes. They make the movie look good. The film crew includes camera operators. They film the movie.

A camera operator listens to the director as she shoots the scenes of a movie.

Sound operators use microphones and other equipment. They record what the actors say.

Lighting **technicians** set up the lights.

They control the lights during filming.

Set designers make sets for the movie. Sets are where the actors act. They are where the movie takes place. A set might be a character's house or office.

Costume designers decide what the actors will wear. Hair and make-up artists help change an actor's look.

Film crew jobs require special skills. Some crew members went to college. Others learn on the job.

A make-up artist reapplies an actor's make-up during a break from filming.

CHAPTER 5

FILM
Editors

Camera operators always film more than is needed for the movie. Film **editors** look at everything that was recorded. It takes a lot of time. Editors work long hours.

Editors decide which parts to use. They leave some parts out. They put other parts together. They add the sound and music.

A film editor uses special computer programs for his work.

Film editors must pay attention to small details.

Editors add the **special effects**. Special effects are fake. But they look real. Special effects might add a monster into a movie. They might make it look like the actors are in outer space.

Editors and directors work together. The editors must understand the movie's story. They must understand the director's ideas.

Many editors studied film at university. They also learn on the job.

MAKING SPECIAL EFFECTS

Some special effects artists use computers. Others use puppets or make-up. They want to make everything look real.

Many different people work in movies. Together they create the movies you watch.

Everyone on a film crew works together as a team.

Do you like watching movies? Do you want to see a story that you wrote on screen? Or do you want to act? You might like to work in movies!

GLOSSARY

agent
person who does business for someone else

audition
short performance given by a performer to see if they are good enough to be in a movie

composer
person who writes music

credits
list of people who worked on a movie

director
person who is in charge of actors and crew members for a movie

editor
person who puts together parts of a movie

lines
parts of the script that the actors say out loud

producer
person who manages money and other parts of making a movie

rehearsal
time to practise acting before filming a movie

rights
permission to use a story to make a movie

role
character that an actor plays

scene
part of a movie

script
written form of a movie, including lines for actors

special effects
images or sounds created to show imaginary things

technician
person who uses machines or technology for their job

FIND OUT MORE

Want to learn more about the movies? Check out these resources:

Books

Make a Film! (Find Your Talent), Jim Pipe (Franklin Watts, 2014)

Smartphone Movie Maker, Bryan Michael Stoller (Walker Books, 2016)

Website

nationalcareersservice.direct.gov.uk/job-profiles/performing-arts-broadcast-and-media
This website tells you about many jobs in movies and TV. Ask an adult or use a dictionary to help you understand any difficult words.

Place to visit

National Science and Media Museum, Bradford
www.scienceandmediamuseum.org.uk
Learn more about cinema at this museum.

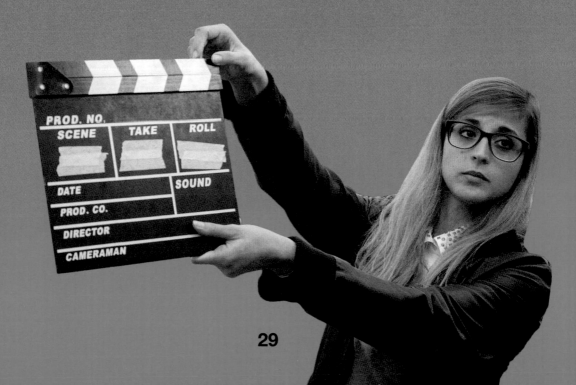

ACTIVITY

MAKE A MOVIE!

All you need is a camera. You can use the camera on a mobile phone or tablet.

Decide what type of movie you will make. Will it be an adventure story or a mystery? Will it be a scary movie? Maybe it will be based on a true story. Write the script. Next, find your actors. They may be friends or family members. Maybe the star is your pet!

You are the director. Tell the actors what you want them to do. Ask them to practise the scenes. When everyone is ready, they can get into their costumes. Time to start filming!

INDEX